MW00629100

73

OH, TERRIBLE YOUTH

BY CRISTIN O'KEEFE APTOWICZ

A Write Bloody Book
Long Beach, CA USA

Oh, Terrible Youth
a collection of poetry

ﬆ

by Cristin O'Keefe Aptowicz

Write Bloody Publishing
America's Independent Press

Long Beach, CA

writebloody.com

Copyright © Cristin O'Keefe Aptowicz

No part of this book may be used or performed without written consent from the author, if living, except for critical articles or reviews.

Aptowicz, Cristin O'Keefe.
1ˢᵗ edition.
ISBN: 978-1-935904-66-3

Interior Layout by Lea C. Deschenes
Cover Designed by Joshua Grieve
Proofread by Sarah Kay
Edited by Derrick Brown and Sarah Kay
Author Photo by Alex Brook Lynn
Type set in Helvetica by Linotype and Bergamo (www.theleagueofmoveabletype.com)

Special thanks to Lightning Bolt Donor, Weston Renoud

Printed in Tennessee, USA

Write Bloody Publishing
Long Beach, CA
Support Independent Presses
writebloody.com

To contact the author, send an email to writebloody@gmail.com

OH, TERRIBLE YOUTH

THIRD AND LAST

When I was born, the disruption caused
my brother to protest, lobbing endless arcs
of shoes into my crib. Squinting, he says

he can still remember a time before me.
Mom often jokes that after having a boy
and a girl, the next logical step would've

been to get a golden retriever. But instead
I arrived: a shrill pudge forever destined
to be the yellow crayon in my mother's

Halloween costume idea. Home videos
show I was a child in a persistent state
of moping, my wide eyes always teary

and on the lookout for gross injustice.
These injustices, or at least those that
were recorded on film, include:

having my birthday candles cruelly
blown out by my older sister repeatedly
on my third birthday; being viciously

knocked over in an inexplicable hula
contest on our front lawn; and a walk
of shame after I peed in my ironically

yellow snowsuit during the annual
Christmas tree hunt. Today, when
friends look through old photo albums,

they have trouble finding me. It's easy,
I say, just look for the one purposefully
having no fun, the one with the bad

self-given haircut, the one crying over
her ugly jack-o-lantern, the one whose
pout seems suspiciously practiced,

the one that looks like the answer
to the question: *Come on, how bad
could having one more kid be?*

MY ELEMENTARY SCHOOL CONFESSIONS

I never finished my year-end final report on Apartheid,
and by *never finished*, I mean never even started.

For a whole year, I made fun of a kid because his lunch mat
showcased the brief biographies of every U.S. President,

despite the fact that I had a proximity-based crush on him,
and that honestly, I'd kill to have that lunch mat now.

While my friends did their oral reports on, no joke,
the RFK assassination conspiracy and the mating songs

of humpback whales, I phoned it in with two reports
on the only things I cared about: dogs and Bigfoot.

My teacher only agreed to these topics, I'm sure,
because she thought it would bring some passion

and actual effort to my work. It did not. In the first grade,
I kicked a kid named Dennis in the nuts so frequently,

his mother had a conversation with me during library time.
In the second grade, I broke a two-foot tall Virgin Mary statue

which belonged to my teacher: a catholic nun named Mary.
In the third grade, I constantly ate the plastic buttons

off my shirts, just hoping I'd get sick. In the fourth grade,
my entire book report on *James and the Giant Peach*

was really just one long run-on sentence and somehow
I still got an "A." In the fifth grade, I told my classmates

my *Sunflowers* repro on canvas was a real Van Gogh.
In the sixth grade, I had the whole school pray for my dad

who was missing in the San Francisco earthquake,
when in reality, he was safe in his hotel lobby in Oakland,

organizing businessmen to make rounds to all
the local powerless restaurants, offering to eat

their melting ice cream and defrosting shrimp cocktails.
It took years for people to stop thinking he was dead.

THIS MASK IS WHAT'S HOLDING MY FACE UP

The first and only year
that the neighborhood dads took
the kids out trick-or-treating

was also the only year that
an open Budweiser keg was
dragged around behind us
in a red Radio Flyer wagon.

It soon became the only Halloween
when us kids were encouraged
to tell people when their candy *sucked,*
or that pennies in a bag didn't cut it;

the only Halloween when
we were allowed to punch jerks
who tried to scare us with
the old *I'm just a mummy sitting
by the candy bowl* trick;

the only Halloween when,
if we ran into the cemetery
and stayed there for 30 seconds,
we were allowed to take whatever
we wanted from the other kids' bags,
even if, and especially if,
it was that kid's favorite candy;

the only Halloween when
we were allowed to switch costumes
and trick or treat at the same house
two or three times because
the candy was good or because
the owner was a *sonuvabitch*;

the only Halloween when,
if you saw a dog dressed up
in a Philadelphia Eagles jersey,
you had to take a shot:

Jack Daniels for the dads,
Extra Sour Warheads for the kids,

and neither one was allowed
to spit it out.

ABSOLUTE WORST LAST MINUTE COSTUMES OF HALLOWEEN

Birthday Present:
Ingredients
Large box around torso
Several rolls of mismatched wrapping paper
Harried mother becoming increasingly impatient
with your whining about how crappy the costume looks

Santa Claus:
Ingredients
Dad's oversized Santa outfit
Lingering stench of sweat and spilled booze
General sense of surreal holiday displacement

Homemade Ewok:
Ingredients
Bristly doormats tied to chest and back with twine
Grandma's fuzzy hat
Whiskers and black nose
Beige purse
Determined denial about how awful this really looks
Tons of bonus candy scored through pity

POLLY WANTS A CRACKER

The waiting room of my childhood dentist's office had two things in it: a stand-up arcade version of Dig-Dug that you didn't need any quarters to play, and a giant red parrot.

My dentist likely assumed that this would pretty much cover all the possible bases of entertaining his tyke patients. If you liked video games, you could play a video game or watch someone else play a video game. And if you didn't like video games, you were clearly dimwitted, so please talk to this old creepy parrot.

The parrot knew one word: *NO!*

But that didn't stop us kids from surrounding his cage and whispering dirty words we hoped he'd learn. Whenever the receptionist noticed us pressing our fat faces against the bars, all huskily whispering, *Fuck! Fuck! Fuck! Fuck!* while the bird shrieked back, *No! No! No! No!* she'd decide to toss in a sad plate of orange slices and peanuts. After this, we'd just have to be content with watching the parrot eat with his scaly dinosaur claws and slimy black tongue.

Hi, my name is Polly, its sign said, *I love to talk! Please don't put your fingers in my cage and always remember to brush and floss your teeth!*

Years later, while watching a PBS nature documentary, I learned parrots are not native to dentists' offices, but rather to the Amazon. They are highly intelligent and can learn hundreds of words. They can live for decades and, when threatened, they can attack, beaks ripping into flesh, diseases injected into their enemies' skin by their own piercing claws.

Parrots are, apparently, beautiful, complex and dangerous birds. Albeit, ones that can easily be distracted by orange slices; ones

that might mistake the start-up music of Dig-Dug for a mating
call, which would explain all the horny hopping; ones that likely
hate children, that don't want to learn to say *Shit* or *Fuck*, but wish
someone would teach it:

Stop playing that blasted game!

or

Stick your fingers in this cage, fat boy, I dare you!

or

*If it were not for this tiny wire door, I would consume your face like a piece
of overripe fruit, tear into your nose like it was an enormous boiled peanut.
Forget that doctor, kid, let me be the one to pull every tooth out of your rotten
little head!*

THE YOUNGEST KID LAMENT, OR MOPING AT THE CROSSROADS

Has anybody written a blues song about hand-me-downs, about how horribly misshapen and unflattering they can be? How ripped jeans are only cool if you buy them ripped, and not because your sister had to cut out the inky blue name of some no-goodnik boy who she doesn't even like anymore?

Is there a blues song that I can listen to that mentions Wedgies? Or Indian Burns? Or Noogies? Or Purple Nurples? Or Wet Willies? Or Swirlies? Or Punchbuggies? Or Tattlers? Or whatever it's called when the car makes a sharp turn and you get mashed into the side of the car like gum into the unpopular kid's hair?

Has there ever been a blues song where the singer is accompanied by shameful disillusionment and unrelenting jealousy?

I bet if there was, the blues singer would have noticeably crooked teeth, because the family conveniently ran out of money for braces by the time it was his turn, and therefore in every Christmas picture from then on, the blues singer would look like the gnarly goat next to the Chicklet-straight smiles of his infinitely luckier siblings.

I wonder if there is a blues song about counting how many times you appear in your family photo albums to prove your point about being ignored? And if there is a blues song about the parental apathy which greets the self-justifying but ultimately depressing results?

And how about someone recording a blues song about hating to share? About how sitting on top of someone and tickling them until they pee themselves is *not* funny? About how everyone else's birthday cakes always taste so much better, their Christmas gifts are so much bigger and more expensive and better thought out than yours?

Me? I'm going to write a blues song about what happens to a whine deferred: How it dries up like an old banana in a closet which your older sister agrees to pay you two dollars to remove from her room, and when you try to remove it, a swarm of black gnats rushes your face and flies into your nose and into your eyes, and your sister yells from the other side of the room, *The worst part is over! Just stick it in the trash bag, stick it in the trash bag!*

And you do, and run outside with it, gagging on gnats, and when you go back to her room, you find the door locked and you bang on it, and your sister says it's no use, she's not paying you, she doesn't have the two dollars anyway, and you bang louder, and then your mother yells at YOU for being too loud, and you go to your mom like a crybaby, and tell her the whole buggy saga, and she tells you to stop blubbering and get over it, that you got what you deserve for trusting your sister, who the whole family knows is a liar.

And your sister, who has been listening through the floorboards, actually goes, *HA-HA!*

THE ABSOLUTE WORST GAMES OF CHILDHOOD

Cemetery
House, if you are anyone but The Mom
The *Let's See Who Can Be the Quietest* Game
The *Let's Try Not to Annoy Dad While the Game's On* Game
Regular Battleship when all your friends have Electronic Battleship
Fifty-Two Pick-Up
Clean-Up Robot
Games in Which You Learn the Capitals of States

8/8/88

It was August 1988, and my family and I were on vacation at Virginia Beach. I was nine, and this may or may not have been the year I boycotted the ocean, tearing through a stack of books under an enormous umbrella. My pale skin, a statement: I don't belong with this family.

We always vacationed in state parks. I remember evenings lying in bed, climbing my feet up the cinderblock walls, the relentless cicadas overpowering the radio my sister had carefully smuggled in. My rebellious older sister: the one who took off alone down the beach for hours, the one who would sometimes refuse to acknowledge me as her sister in front of tan boys with popped collars, the one who seemed endlessly attracted to the payphone at the park's Welcome Center and the Philadelphia boys all tied up at the other end of it.

All the local radio station DJs kept barking about the importance of that summer: August 8, 1988 was going to be 8/8/88, a lining up of numbers we wouldn't see again until September 9th, 1999, 9/9/99: a decade from now, a lifetime from now. I did the math, figured I'd be in college by then, maybe in New York City, certainly not pale and nine and stuck in Virginia Beach.

The night of 8/8/88, my parents took us for an evening picnic to watch the sun go down over Chesapeake Bay. I wanted so desperately to do something memorable, sure that children, or grandchildren, or maybe just distant interviewers, would ask what I did on the night of 8/8/88. Instead, I pouted and sighed, watched my family smear tubbed cheese on crackers. I could feel the heat radiating off their sunburnt bodies.

I admit to you now: I never once thought about my parents, who pushed hard at their government jobs all year to afford these two weeks in an un-air-conditioned cabin. I didn't think about my bony brother and sister, poised to dive into their own lives, swimming away from me and my small pale protests. Never thought of our family, the five of us, as anything other than five fingers on the same hand; never thought of us as water in a thrashing river, ready to divide.

No, that night, all I thought about was myself, dry on all that damp sand, absolutely unspectacular. Another night I would never remember, I thought, as the stars began poking their fingers through the clouds, dragging night behind them: not even one comet, not even a half of burning meteorite, not one single special thing to remember. Nothing, I thought, not one thing.

UNLIKELY WAYS
I WAS CONVINCED I WAS GOING TO DIE
(AND THE MOVIES THAT
INSPIRED THESE THOUGHTS)

Eaten by a Shark While Taking a Bath
(*Jaws*)

Knife-covered Glove Through the Chest While Sleeping
(*Nightmare on Elm Street*)

Stabbed in the Neck by Santa Claus
(*Silent Night, Deadly Night*)

Brain Eaten by Bug Placed in My Ear
(*Star Trek II: Wrath of Khan*)

Chased by Jack Nicholson Through a Snowy Garden Maze
(*The Shining*)

Boredom
(*Somewhere in Time*)

AT THE ST. CHRISTOPHER
6TH GRADE DANCE

For G., wherever you may be

I remember the parting of bodies, as if the shock
registered first in the soles of shiny new shoes.
They reeled. It was then that I caught sight of you,

the most unpopular boy in the class,
in the center of the dance floor, paused,
glittering with anticipation, and then: BOOM!

Your body hit that beat, or maybe it was the beat
that hit your body, you jolted into precision.
BOOM BOOM BOOM! Your body was fired up

and expectant. Until that moment, I'm sure
the popular boys thought they owned the floor
with their earrings and clear skin. But then,

your song arrived and you fell into legend:
the kid who could dance. You spun around
like hip-hop itself, drilling into 80's culture.

Your face: frozen, concentrated. Your limbs
snapping on beat, BOOM BOOM BOOM!
All around you, staring, were your classmates,

whom you must have hated. I hated them.
I was as unpopular as you, but I had been given
the opportunity to escape, one day a week

taking classes in the public school, my mother
insisting that I get that raucous perspective:
learn that there were races other than white,

religions other than Christian, girls other than these
cruel and beautiful pocket knives, these sharp
silver spoons gagging already skinny throats.

That night, I watched you, impressed as the rest.
The DJ grinning. BOOM BOOM BOOM!
I know I wanted to do more than just clap,

more than just join the crowd in shouting
your name, a brief moment when you might
have actually felt accepted. Looking back,

if I could be anything, I would be that strobe light,
spontaneously lit by the DJ, shattering its light
across you, christening you into something better.

Making it appear for a brilliant moment,
that you were more than your body,
that you didn't even have to be here.

That given the sweet hot opportunity,
that maybe you would just go ahead and—
BOOM BOOM BOOM!— *explode*.

WHAT NO ONE EVER TELLS YOU ABOUT PUGS

Did you know that the shallow eye sockets
and flattened faces of pugs make it very easy
for their eyeballs to just pop out? They don't
tell you stuff like that, like they don't mention
that the genes that make Dalmatians so spotted
are also what makes them deaf, or that Bulldogs
are delivered by C-section, or that Cocker Spaniels
are known to lapse into uncontrolled fits of anger.
Really, it's called "The Cocker Rage Syndrome."
Try to find stuff like this in books. You can't.

I found out about the pug thing through a real life
experience. When we were kids, my friend David
once accidentally closed the bathroom door
on the head of his aunt's pug, and its eyeball popped
right out. To make matters worse, it was Christmas,
and the vet couldn't save the eye. They brought
the dog home heavily sedated, wearing a cone collar
and large button over its newly emptied socket.
The family then ate Christmas dinner. Poor Dave,
he couldn't stop crying, guilty and young at the table,
and everyone said not to be so upset, that it was
an accident, that it could have happened to anyone.

Everyone except the aunt, who glared at him
with her two good and narrow eyes, and me,
who could not stop laughing when he called me
from the guest bedroom, tear-soaked and throaty.
He made me promise not to laugh, but I did anyway.
Who knew such a thing was possible? I mean, really.
It's not like they tell you this stuff in books.

LITERAL PORTRAIT OF THE WRITER AS A TWELVE-YEAR-OLD

Brendan Rosenberg became a man in 1991, and the theme of his journey into manhood was *Star Trek*.

You were able to figure out pretty quickly what he thought of you by the seating arrangement. His best friends joined him at the table labeled, *The Enterprise*. His parents and grandparents were seated at *Starfleet Academy*. My placard could be found at *Klingon Ship #2*, which may well have been called *Extra Invitations*. I was thrilled.

When you are twelve, which I was, and you are a straight girl, which I also was, the entire population of males from two years younger than you to several years older proffer themselves to your heart unwittingly. Men who read this, please know: no matter how you may have felt you looked in middle school, I guarantee that you were the object of several crushes—albeit some as brief as a math period.

Brandon Rosenberg, with his enormous woolly head, rubbery lips, and baleful grey eyes, was no exception. In fact, his bar mitzvah was flooded with boys who made me as jittery as a knee, who—with one slow dance—could have had my heart, my brain, and anything else above the clothes for the taking.

But instead, all I received was a caricature.

I had the misfortune of having mine done directly after Nicole A., the gorgeous blond goy of our grade. She requested to be drawn as a princess, the effect completed by her own real live court of fawning teen boys. They were delirious with the opportunity to be able to stare at her as long as they wanted, saliva collecting in their braces, yarmulkes becoming damp with excitement.

The finished product was radiant, pink and perfect. The boys actually applauded. The caricaturist did a little half bow.

There was a mass exodus when Nicole left, and the caricaturist actually let out a sigh before he turned to me and asked me how I would like to be drawn.

I want to be drawn as a writer, I responded.

He stared at me and let out another sigh.

To be fair, "Writer" is probably more difficult to draw than the triangle hat of "Princess," or the goofy oval and action lines of "Tennis Player." For writer, there would likely have to be a desk drawn, a chair, a typewriter. The caricaturist fidgeted.

Well, he fished, *Okay… um, what kind of things do you write?*

Anything! Everything! I lied, dramatically, *Short stories… Poetry… Plays…*

His eyes lit up.

Like a BROADWAY play? He asked.

I remember this: my hair was painful with hairspray, the too tight dress I wore was my sister's, and no one told me or my dirty feet that it was in fashion to bring your own white socks in which to dance.

I'm embarrassed to say I remember my clumpy mascara-ed eyes stinging as I looked off past the caricaturist's shoulder: the first slow dance of the afternoon and no one was even glancing my way.

I remember thinking that this would all make a terrible poem.

Done! the caricaturist cheerfully said, and presented me with what is still framed in my apartment, a young me with wild permed hair and a strained enormous smile, wearing a gold body suit, high heels and fishnets, carrying a gold top hat and matching gold cane.

I am kicking one leg up in the air, staring directly at the viewer, as if to say:

Yes, look! Look at me! For what am I, if I am not the very picture of a writer.

HOW I SPENT MY SUMMER VACATIONS

Eating my own weight in microwave pizza.

Not getting kissed.

Forgetting basic math skills.

Loathing movies featuring girls who go to horse camp, especially if those girls get kissed.

OUR YEAR OF SMUT

Even now, the line slouches conspiratorially in my chest,
my education's first dirty joke, dark and perfect as a plum,
the glittering moment my pants told my head, *A-ha!*

The professor had asked if we knew what Hamlet meant,
when after his offer to lay on her lap was rejected,
he asked Ophelia, *Do you think I meant country matters?*

And us, clean-haired, in our first month of senior year, dipped
our toes in the water of indecency. *Could Shakespeare be
making a metaphor: country meaning farm meaning fertile...?*

Our professor squinted at us, *It's much easier than all that,*
and we stared, blankly patient, pressing our fingers together,
waiting. *Country*, he said, *he's talking about her <u>cunt</u>.*

The room was suddenly white with silence. My heart:
a dark squid pulsating lustily, ink leaking behind it. Maybe
he knew what he was doing, that this one sentence would

make us gulp down each book cleaver-close, this classroom
of virgins told that Shakespeare had meant *cunt*, the closed
fists of our sex divining meaning from nothing, the professor

unsuccessfully trying to get us to back off our theories
that the cows in *Tess of the d'Urbervilles* were clear symbols
of lesbianism, that Oliver Twist and the Artful Dodger were

obviously lovers, that every cracked door, every heaving dusk,
every boat left floating at chapter's end held the barely hidden
clues of slippery animal sex. The boring baroque language was

a knotty pine wall and it was our job to find the peephole
and it was always there, always. The professor would wipe
his moist brow, learn to close the door before the start of class,

and we'd wait for him, legs jiggling, chewing on pens,
as he sat on his desk's edge, rubbing his temple with a meaty
hand, already regretting putting *Moby Dick* on his syllabus.

FACTS ABOUT SEVEN U.S. PRESIDENTS I STILL SOMEHOW REMEMBER AND THE COMPLETELY AWFUL YET SURPRISINGLY EFFECTIVE WAYS I REMEMBERED THEM

Franklin Pierce helped pass the Kansas–Nebraska Act
which rendered useless the Missouri Compromise,
thus hastening the advent of the Civil War.

> *"Franklin doth Pierce the Missouri Compromise
> with his Kansas-Nebraska Axe! There will be Civil War!"*

Andrew Johnson was the only Southern Senator not to secede.

> *"What, you aren't seceding with us?
> Johnson, you're a dick!"*

James A. Garfield was the last president born in a log cabin.

> *Picture cartoon cat Garfield sleeping in a log cabin.*

Martin van Buren's nickname was O.K.
(stands for Old Kinderhook, where he grew up.)

> *If the Van (Buren) is a rocking,
> it's O.K. coming a-knocking.*

Chester A. Arthur was very well-dressed
and earned the nickname "The Gentleman Boss."

> *Picture pervy guy in a ritzy white suit going,
> "Hi... I'm Chessssster."*

Millard Fillmore married his teacher.

"Millard, I want to fill your brain with more knowledge"
"Good, 'cause I want to fill your p*ssy with more c*ck."

Herbert Hoover was orphaned at the age of nine.

"Both your parents are dead and you're nine?
Hoover, it <u>sucks</u> to be you."

THE SECRET LANGUAGE OF NERDS

Around the time we learned about negative functions in our algebra classes, a group of us began talking differently.

You're cooler than me, we'd say, *to the natural log.*

Which meant that you were inversing the statement, which meant the speaker was actually the cooler one, unless, that is, if you were to retort,

I totally agree, but only if you also mean to the power of negative one,

which flipped the statement again, meaning the speaker was the less cool one.

And everyone would laugh if they got the joke, and if you got the joke, it meant that you were in. Not the typical high school *in*, no, the physical *in*: inside, indoors, in your room studying to the sounds of French pop, because you heard that made learning French easier.

Our favorite French phrase was *J'ai dit ça pour rigoler*, which loosely translates to *I'm kidding* but actually translates to *I said that in order for you to laugh*, which is infinitely funnier and more passive aggressive than our own dumb English.

French was the one thing that didn't come easily to us, which is to say that nothing really comes easy. We worked. Hard. But French was the thing that we couldn't overcome, something we couldn't translate into our working class lives, no matter what horrendous music we listened to.

The weekend before the A.P. test we decided that our brains were fixed, stubborn, and the only way we were going to succeed is if we pretended we were smarter than our brains would let us be. We furiously created and memorized our fake smart phrases, meticulously repeating, *Oh no, the tape player must be broken* in French for the oral portion of the test, copying the phrase, *Oh no, the words on this page are all smeared!* in French for the essay.

We deluded ourselves into thinking that if several people complained of technical problems, that would make it more believable.

But to cover our tails, we each independently studied vocabulary words, unusual words we hoped would make us seem worldly and authentic when recorded.

I committed to memory more than a dozen words related to being artistic and being goth, hoping that my salvation would lay in the lack of overlap: how many nerdy artistic Goths could possibly be taking A.P. French tests in Philadelphia that year?

Of course, it didn't work. We were slapped with 3s, and forced to take French again in college. *Merde.*

And at first, we felt like bad crooks, but as the years passed, those 3s became badges of honor, proof that there was that fabled fine line between clever and stupid, and that we were capable of being that line.

We were nerds, sure, but we were teenagers; we could say *J'ai dit ça pour rigoler* and mean it.

The vocabulary words have faded; the flashcards, lost; the language remains absolutely unlearned, I can still puff out my chest at the spectacular truth: I was a nerdy goth poet who tried, who at least tried, to be her very best in French and maybe even succeeded in her own small way.

After all, I have to imagine that there was a smile, if not a full and honest laugh, when the underpaid AP Test reader came to the "Tell the Story" portion of my test.

What other student colored in the outfit of the lead cartoon jogger: an all-black penciled-in attire? What other student, in a last attempt to salvage her test, had the injured jogger fall to his side, dramatically cry out to the heavens:

Oh God, Why? Why did you give me this dark passion for running? It has become a terrible curse to me now!

HIGH FASHION

Vanessa dragged forks across her stockings
to create the perfect runs. She'd sometimes wear
two at a time—black on black, black on red—
so slim, I can't believe we once shared cardigans.

Kim based her junior prom outfit on the scene
in *Sid and Nancy* where Sid Vicious shoots
an entire audience of well-dressed concert-goers.
Nancy wakes up, bloody and bulleted, to smile.

Julianna did not seem from my world at all.
Hair always blue or bright purple, I don't know
where she found her clothes, or how she could
afford them, or why she would even speak to me,

dressed as I was. I admit, sometimes I'd fantasize
someone would die, leave me their complicated boots,
their fitted velvet jackets and studded leather jewelry.
That luck (and death) would have me strutting

in some high fashion. But instead, everyone just
kept living, including me. So I stumbled through
school in a steady stream of flannel, cotton and
corduroys. Thrift store shirts that probably looked

cool when new, when black, but had long since
faded into an absolutely unremarkable gray.

BENEDICTION FOR PROM NIGHT

Lord, we first ask for protection of the self:
that the dress still fits,
that the make-up isn't smeared,
that the hair doesn't act up,
that the shoes don't rub,
that the breath don't stink,
that the nails don't break,
that the breasts stay where they should,
that this hard-earned vision
remains steadfastly perfect.

Lord, next we ask for blessings on the night:
that the date arrives,
that the corsage isn't tacky,
that the parents don't embarrass,
that the car isn't a hoopty,
that the sky doesn't pour,
that the friends aren't idiots,
that the music isn't horrible,
that the table doesn't wobble,
that the water stays in the glass,
that the food stays on the plate,
that our favorite song doesn't start
when we're in the bathroom.

And Lord, lastly we pray for us,
that we recognize the unconscious beauty of youth,
that we feel the fleeting heat of a slow song,
that we listen to the soft hum of the present,
that we see our future, with its hand out, impatient,
but choose to hold on and dance a little longer.

ESTEPHANIA

Maybe it was my habitually dirty mouth,
or my habitually dirty hair, or maybe it was
the way cockiness and bragging would prop
their charcoal feet on my irises, mindlessly
stoking the haughty fire of my tongue.

Maybe it was my childhood's lack of ribbons
and Barbies, my zeal at being the only kid
ghoulish enough to slice meaty nightcrawlers
with my thumbnail for perching on dad's hook,
but whatever it was, I saw myself as a boy's girl.

I didn't know what to do with myself when
visiting with female friends: their canopy beds,
their ceramic harlequin masks, their photo albums
made of puffy fabric and glitter paint. Their mothers
sensed my wildness, nervously handing me

tumblers of iced tea destined to be knocked over,
the relentless jitter of limbs, my dirty nails,
the unforgivably sorry mess of me. In the fifth grade,
we met: two pudgy collections of fashion mistakes,
two braying sacks of girl giggles and buck teeth,

and God gave you the impossible task of guiding
me through to womanhood, our friendship tugging me
together when my mouth exploded all over itself,
the gentle counsel of your eyes, the generous salve
of your laugh, the unintentional comedy of our hair.

Our teen years read like a satire on unloveablity,
our diaries like racing forms just trying to keep up
with the latest of our galloping, resistible hearts.

There were years when we were never kissed,
there were boys who'd threatened the tender

sinews of our shared self, times we wanted
to shatter the mirror of each other's bodies:
I am not you! I could never ever be you!
and yet here we are. Almost twenty years later:
full grown and fleshed out, with love finally

sleeping sweetly in our own beds. On Sunday,
we shared perhaps our millionth meal, banging
our laughs together like ceremonial gongs, and
I marveled at the startling women who sprouted
from such riotous, unstoppable and perfect girls.

A SESTINA ABOUT TEENAGE LOVE
AS INSPIRED BY E.E. CUMMINGS

i / love / you / and / only / you!

you / and i / only! / i love / you and / you!

you! / you! / and / i / love / only

only / you! / i love / you! / i / and

i and / only / i / love you! / you / love

love! / and / you, / only / you / love i!

you love / only i and / i love only you!

APOLOGIES TO MY CHILDHOOD DOG

I'm sorry about the time I thought
that you'd enjoy the ocean more
if you just got past the breakers,
your nervous nostrils twitching,
how I abandoned you when I saw
that first big wave approaching.

I'm sorry about the attention I paid
to that stray kitten we kept for a week
in the attic, and how that tenderness
was eventually repaid to you in fleas.

I'm sorry that I would laugh
every time they would shave you
for the summer, the shocked ladies
at the grooming shop clucking at me,
Don't laugh! Don't laugh!
He'll know you're laughing at him!

I'm sorry that I would strip you
of your holiday neckerchiefs
whenever my mom left for work,
letting my own goth embarrassment
outweigh your obvious love
of wearing them, your flag
of a tail waving every time
Mom put one on.

But most of all, I'm sorry
I didn't write you more poems
when you were alive:

the pads of your feet kicked out
over linoleum, the pink dangle
of your happy tongue, the way
you'd speed through piles
of crisp leaves,

a happy brown blur, here,
then gone.

TIMES I WISH I WERE FUNNIER

Every day.

HEAVENLY CREATURE
for Missy

I remember the day you showed up at the bus stop:
quiet, pale, a thick veil of dark hair; we stared

at each other through overgrown bangs. We were just
beginning our dry sentences at Baldi Middle School.

In those days, our jeans would be tattooed weekly
with the coded names of every boy who flicked

his eyes our way. The backs of our hands became
necks and lips for practicing on. I once even

doused my backpack with my brother's cologne,
a sad effort to at least smell like I had a boyfriend.

Walking around your housing complex, we'd stare
through the windshields of every man who drove by.

We thought of our bodies as dangerous chemicals,
our breasts as match tips waiting for love's flinty gaze.

We were sure all the boys around had firecracker hearts
just waiting to explode. And look, I know I know I know

I am not telling the whole truth. Things in your house
were different, were not right, were accepted because

maybe no one knew any better, or maybe they did
and didn't care. And whenever the whole dark truth

would spill out, I remember I'd gather my features
into the center of my face, unable to figure out

the right combination for my concern, for fresh alarm.
I'd forget how to sit, how to blink, breathe. It's true,

sometimes you look back and all the things
you should have done rise up like volcanic islands,

whole civilizations, whole existences, whole lifetimes.
But what did we know then? Fourteen, I took

the hammer of my dumb tongue and tried to tap
comfort into your impossibly small ears,

your impossibly small fists. We were kids,
and the future was our dependable escape plan.

We'd be gone soon, so you had just better suffer through
it all now. We'd be gone, so until then, I tried

to make you laugh. I'm sorry I never realized
I could've unlocked your exit earlier, that I

could've released your story from the shotgun
of my own throat. The letters you send me now

are like postcards from that hopeful future:
you are okay, you are alright, with no return address.

So this poem is a telegram to let you know that
I still think about you, that I'm still proud of you,

that when I remember you, I always remember you
as beautiful.

I KNOW WE CAN NEVER LOOK BACK
for D.C.H.

Your bedroom was a box spring
on the floor, clothing in milk crates,
Doors lyrics scotch-taped to the walls.

You said your parents' theory was
to buy all the nice furniture before moving,
so when you could finally afford

a nice house in a nice neighborhood,
you wouldn't be embarrassed to invite
people inside. They never took

into consideration that people might steal
nice furniture in a poor neighborhood,
or that parents might just need to resell it

to make rent in an area that had no shame
in tossing people out on the street.
I remember being embarrassed

of my own family's house in winter,
when we dialed down the heat to save money,
and friends could see their own breath.

Air was free, so we didn't have a dryer,
and in cold weather, our pants and towels
would steep in the smell of our basement.

All my hand-me-downs, all the pens
and staplers lifted from the government,
all the generic cereal bought in bulk,

I remembered wanting to have things
just a little easier, just a little, just a little.
The only time you let me see

where you lived, your mother made us
mac and cheese with sliced hot dogs.
You showed me around, tight-mouthed,

and kept careful watch of the window:
I had to be back on the train before dark.
On the El ride home, I didn't even try

to find your house from above. In fact,
I wished I'd never seen your place, never
spent those sunny afternoons comparing

our stories, amazed that we were so similar.
It was obvious I knew nothing, my heart
shuddering safe in its cage. I thought back

to how we'd collect pennies together, sure
of their worth, the tee-shirts we'd purchase
by the pound, how sometimes we'd pool

our money to buy a whole pizza just for us,
just for us, this is just for us and let's promise
we won't share it with anyone else.

THE UNREACHABLE END OF HIGH SCHOOL

There were times I'd lie on my bedroom floor
for hours, sure I could feel time absolutely stop.
This was the power of my heartbreak.

There was no music dramatic enough to score
my bus rides home from school: heart swelling,
eyes moist, his name, his name, his name.

I trembled with possibility. The things I touched
and tasted, the things I wanted so very badly,
each night's dark sweet potential: it was dizzying.

If I was confident of one thing, it was that this all
would never change: my startling maturity,
the way I'd see myself in a mirror, the grace

of night spilling onto street, summer walks home,
how much I'd swoon at the smell of unwashed hair.
I was sure all that was gritty and smooth, all that

was the foundation of me, would be there. Always.
It was given. It was too much. And there were times
I could hardly stand it.

IGNITION

like the first time you step
into the driveway and see no parents

the first time you open that door
and the sound it makes when you close it

the first time you hear the rebel's yell of your engine
and the buzzing confederacy it stirs in your ribs

the first time you leave the neighborhood
and the whole city explodes onto your radar

and you could go anywhere, anywhere,
and the radio feels like a soundtrack

and the radio feels like an anthem

STARLING

I read a poem about a starling and thought,
I want to write a poem about a starling.
Then I remembered: I don't think I've ever
seen a starling. In fact, my fuzzy vision
of them is largely based on tattoos,

which I'm not even convinced are starlings.
They could be hummingbirds, or blackbirds,
or even trustworthy, boring old sparrows,
for all I know. I always thought I had

a fairly rural upbringing, but that was mostly
because I grew up in Philly and not NYC.
Compared to New York City, everything
can seem a little provincial. My first week

in New York City, the RA in our dorm
asked us all to talk about our favorite animals
and list the traits we loved about them.
Afterwards, the RA announced it was a test,

a psychological test, and all those traits we'd
admitted to liking about our favorite animals
were really traits we liked about ourselves.
We all felt a bit tricked, a bit exposed.

I immediately regretted my choice. Why did I
announce my love of the platypus: its webbed
feet and leathery duck bill; its ability to lay eggs
but still nurse its young with warm lapped milk;

the fact that scientists have studied the platypus
for years and still don't know what in the hell
to make of it.

LIST OF AWESOME THINGS YOU HAVE TO DO
(AN ACTUAL LIST I FOUND
IN ONE OF MY OLD JOURNALS)

Make a video starring yourself
Make a book of comics
Write a poem about dating men from specific countries:
    one poem per country
Also, same idea but states
Make an MC Brainiac outfit, for a new nerdy rap character
Do one small self portrait in ink a day in a self-portrait only book
Do portraits of friends on fabric and make a quilt
Take a Polaroid camera and make a book
Collect rocks that look like your friends
Make a mix tape that will make guys fall in love with you
Make a big book of correspondence
More funny poems
One cussless week
Make money to buy food and clothing

THINGS I SWORE I'D DO
WHEN I WAS GROWN-UP

Eat as much frosting as I wanted everyday (age 3)
Have three kids and name them Tic, Tac, and Toe (age 5)
Have three dogs named Holly, Jogger, and Austin (age 7)
Become famous for painting watercolors of the seashore (age 8)
Move to Nebraska (age 10, shortly after receiving a perfect score on
    my state report on Nebraska)
Wear combats under my dress for all formal affairs (age 15)
Write screenplays starring protagonists with names that only started
    with Q (age 16)
Never shave my legs (age 17)
Marry somone known for being sensible, preferably a scientist (age 19)
Take vitamins everyday, no joke, everyday (age 21)
Stop signing letters "mucho love-o" (age 23)
Stop writing about when I was a kid (age 27)

SPRINGTIME IN QUEENS

Every year, the earth gulps down
an entire season of snow, after which
the apple blossoms return to wriggle
their tender petals in the wind.

The relentlessly eager crocuses
poke their heads out of the dirt
like new gold, warm rain gracing
windows like molten silver.

Soon, downy robins will appear,
fanning their velvet feathers,
plopping out perfect eggs so blue,
people name crayons after them.

I walk home to leaves bursting
from every crooked branch,
perfect as jade earrings. I love
this ripening city and its ability

to move on, as if winter was nothing,
a dreary phase, a tedious fad, as if
winter was a pouting ex-lover, one
that she is way better off without.

LILITH

That morning you woke up alone,
small in your empty Brooklyn bed,
forgotten, left behind, my heart
fanned its darkest smile. You,

who had been so cruel, now wearing
your paper dress, your sloppy drunk,
your careful parade of *I'm over it*,
your wither, your ice, your sneer.

The new woman was a laugher,
all ditz and curl, but enough for him
to leave. Though you would be the one
who'd move, claim to be better off

without. Perhaps it was this brashness,
this faux resilience, that had me hold
tight as leather, riding your bucking
heartbreak, as guiltless and flashy

as a weekend cowboy, savoring
each crack with an eager pinkie.
I clung to it like bad voodoo,
like a perfect and deserved hex,

watching your gaunt striving,
your cheek turning, your nose
rubbed in it, the other woman
laughing at the end of the bar.

When curiosity finally made me
take my boot off your throat,
it was then I noticed you weren't
moving. Sober like a face slap,

obvious as the morning after,
I saw you for what you are:
a woman, cruel and imperfect,
a fighter who tried everything

to protect her one and only heart,
how it didn't matter, it was torn
fresh from its root anyway, with
me, standing by, silent, leering.

STARTER MARRIAGE

With love, there is the bright, white, flashbulb moment,
sealed with a kiss, of course, and that marks the slick second
in which a marriage begins. But, friend, you and I have been
tied to each other's hips for years without cake, or bouquet,
and definitely no kiss. *Friendship*, a high school pal once said,
is a ship big enough for one, and I remember tapping his cheek
with my fingers. *Oh, you're such a misanthrope*, I sighed,
sending up my S.A.T. word like a victory flag. But years later,
you make me think of it: the salted wood and pilled sails,
this ship in which I think you sit, while I'm in the water,
pushing. In so many ways, I have felt married to you, felt lucky
to hold course through the choppy waters of your temper,
waited patiently as you visited all those girl-shaped islands
you'd later call mistakes, lashed myself to your hull when
all common sense screamed *mutiny*. Ours is a burnished
friendship, an earned one, and I have felt proud to know
every one of your sailor's knots and how to untie them.
But friend, you are no lover; you are no husband. You
sit on the meaty side of heart and still claim *hunger*.
Drag me up and down the scales of your anger, and still claim
alone. You pin it to me on the sidewalk, a spitty *Fuck you*,
and walk away like you know I'll still follow. It's hard
to know where this is going or maybe how it is going to end.
Friend, please know you are my most exhausted ardor,
my most tested faith, that you taught me what I'd want
to have in a partner by not being it. That when love sat
down across from me in a diner, followed me home
with a soft knapsack of a mouth, utterly emptied
of sharp words, I wept at how easy it all was. Still, friend,
I know that you were here first, that we are something
worth fighting for, but please listen when I tell you
I'm not sure how long I can keep fighting you
in order to save us.

ACCUSED

Within days, our small community stiffed and spiked.
Words got glaringly precise: *assault, penetration, victims.*
Your familiar face stormed our minds and changed shape.

When it was all laid out to me, it seemed something you'd
be stupid enough to do, but I couldn't imagine you'd meant
harm. But who cares if you meant it. It was done. And so,

meetings are held, letters are drafted and passed around,
pledges made, as I try to keep track of it all with a leaking chest.
My partner confesses, *I don't want to know half this stuff.*

Friend says, *Isn't alcoholism the elephant in the room?*
I mean, would stuff like this happen if everyone wasn't
so hell bent on getting trashed all the time?

Still another friend says, *Don't ask why. Just listen.*
So we listen, her thin voice trembling, her eyes
shrugging out hot tears, one by one by one.

LUCK

Some say the only measurement of luck
is life. Others say health. Others claim
those with living parents, living children,
should side themselves with all that is golden.
There should be no complaints from you.
But who here isn't guilty of feeling like luck
has left them aching over small things:
a missed bus, a leaking pen, your boss catching
you at your worst possible moment. Who here
hasn't cursed a smiling face, thinking, *Why do
they have all the luck?* Your Christmas dinner
failing once again, your body not living up
to the standard your mother set for it. And what
of those people who claim luck is what you make?
Oh, how I wish they would die to see if that
would change their grossly sunny outlook. Me?
I get caught in the taffy of perspective. Health
and family intact, I wake up every morning
to a home and to work and to love. And yet
some days, I pout in luck's black cat shadow,
wondering when the capricious finger of fate
will tilt my way. In these moments, I hope
that fortune isn't paid in gratefulness.
Other days though, I can feel luck tapping
on my breastplate—the hope, the unending
hope!—I know each shooting star was made
for me. On these days, my writing comes
on strong, each line, each word, blooming
from my fingers like clovers, poems coming
together like a mirror breaking in reverse.

REMEMBERING THE NIGHT WE MET

At the after party, you bee-lined right to me,
and I assumed that you were interested in Amanda,
that fluorescent light bulb of a girl, long and thin
and luminous, boys buzzing around her like gnats.

I remember thinking you were clever, buttering up
her geeky friend, the one wearing a dress with sneakers,
the one who kept wandering back to the free food,
the one chomping on a plastic cup filled with ice.

You know: me. So I put my full support behind what
I thought was your project, dutifully introducing you
to Amanda again and again and again, waiting
the requisite two minutes, and then politely exiting

so you could work your magic alone. I remember being
frustrated that you kept coming back to me, wondering,
Does this idiot think I am her pimp or something?
It never occurred to me, I swear, that anyone

would be interested in me, when there were so many
other straightforwardly beautiful options in the room:
girls pink and shiny from wine, their easy smiles,
their straight spines, their clean hair.

When you kissed me at the end of the night, a peck
really, it was enough to pull the whole scene in to clarity.
I didn't know what to say, so I just left, your book
damp in my hand. But know this: you were the U

in my stutter and blush. That one kiss making
the empty O in my chest finally go, *Ohhhh.*

SESTINA FOR SHAPPY
WHO DOESN'T GET ENOUGH LOVE POEMS

Who knew that when the fickle finger of love
finally poked my ribs, it would choose you,
a 30-year-old who willingly calls himself Shappy,
a panda-shaped poet so absurd and funny,
when we met I thought you were part cartoon,
a fellow for whom "excess kitsch" defines "home."

The summer I met you, I was making Astoria my home.
Four months out of college, and I had no job, no love,
no prospects, no optimism. My life was a sad cartoon:
Me, a lonely cat waiting for the Pepé Le Peu which was you.
Before I assumed: a scientist, more logical than funny.
It was ridiculous to think I'd date a guy named Shappy.

But that's how you were introduced me, as Shappy.
No one knew your real name, not even in Chicago, your home.
Earliest impression: you were drunk and you were funny.
That was your plan: to make me laugh until I fell in love.
You just hoped I wouldn't fall into the pattern familiar to you:
Women grew up and left; who wanted to marry a cartoon?

And hey, even I was a litte afraid: could I be with a cartoon?
I mean, a non-scientist? A non-office worker? A... Shappy?
But we all know the ending here: I ended up with you.
You left freezing Chicago to make New York City your home
and we ignored all the critics of our dizzying brand of love,
'cause aren't we at our most beautiful when we're just being funny?

In fact, isn't life the most beautiful when it's just being funny?
Who cares if our apartment looks like the set of a cartoon?
And it's not as if we don't make money as well as love:
me as a serious writer and you as the poet named Shappy.
Together we cram dollars into savings so we can buy a home
big enough for all your stuff, the things you love, and you.

But right now, I'm enjoying life as it is for me and you:
the way everything, even the tragedies, can be funny;
the dachshund- and pop culture-filled hovel called home;
the way every day is a new episode of our life's silly cartoon.
This life we live just amazes me, Shappy.
Who thought this would be my definition of love?

I would have never picked you, my beautiful cartoon,
but ain't life funny? After all, it made you, Shappy,
the perfect home for all my heart's dumb dumb love.

FRIENDS OF BOYFRIENDS

Andy had a gland problem. Or something.
He was completely convinced he'd never have
a girlfriend, was frequently barefoot, smoked.

Jon considered himself the biggest druggie
in all of Harrisburg, mostly meaning his parents'
prescription drugs, paint fumes, booze.

Brian knew he was going right into the Marines
after high school. Even got to wear the uniform
to the prom, striking awe in his teen mom date.

Phil was the guy in the school who always wore
a hat. It was his thing. That and being barefoot
and smoking. And yet he hated Andy.

Shag was a serial letch. Paulie thought
he was an actual wizard. Pettus would hit
on your sister, stare at your mom's tits.

Louis was the guy who you felt lucked
into the top of the class. Said things like,
You know, you're smart for a girl,

and really meant it.

THE SCHOOL OF AVOIDING EYE CONTACT

All I can offer is this: *I've been there.*
I know what it's like to want to be done

with it, to want the minutes to cleanly
flip without all that rotten heat,

to turn off every stubborn nerve
which jumps hopeful at his voice.

I've been there in the car, when you are
so sure that it's all going to flood out,

love as inevitable as night, as *this.*
Listen, it never ends how you want,

closure: the itch you'll never reach.
And there isn't a word, or a song,

or a moment that's going to set you free.
But I guarantee this: there will be

a morning when you wake up,
and the day will trudge by without

a single thought of him, and that too
will bring its own sadness.

OLD BOYS

I would've never believed that I'd forget you:
the sound of your laugh, the size of your hands,
that one day I'd have to rub my forehead
like a genie's lamp to pull out your last name.

I would have slit my tender palm to pulp
to shake bloody and swear that one day
we would share a last name, or at least
a flamboyantly oversized prom picture.

But now, I could form a terrible band
with all the boys I thought would pant
their presence forever on my heart, but
instead evaporated almost completely,

leaving only the tease of our nicknames,
the soft ghost of their favorite tee-shirt,
and the dusty ordinary ellipse of what
could have been.

AFTER READING
OLD UNREQUITED LOVE POEMS

If I didn't think it would make me appear crazy still,
I'd apologize to you for having been so crazy then.

Reading the poems I had written about "us"
resurrected all that nervous heat, reminded me

of the insistent stutter of my longing,
how I could never just lay it out there for you.

The answer, clearly, would have been
no, thank you. But perhaps that tough line

would have been enough to salvage all
that was good and woolly about us: your laugh,

that golden ring I'd always stretch a story for;
the pair of mittens we'd split in the cold

so we'd each have a hand to gesture with;
how even now, the paths we took are filled

with starry wonder and all that bright limitless air.
I'm sorry I could never see myself

out of the twitching fever of my heartache,
that I traded everything we had for something

that never ended up being. But if I could take
any of it back, it wouldn't be the glittering hope

I stuck in the amber of your eyes, nor would
it be the sweet eager of our conversations.

No, it would be that last stony path to nothing,
when we both gave up without telling the other.

How silence arrived like a returned valentine,
that morning we finally taught our phones not to ring.

ALL THE SMALL THINGS

Every year, the acorns drop
from the oaks near the playground,
and every year the kids gasp.

They had forgotten, of course,
as the previous seasons brought
their own dark joys: the snowballs

of winter, the dandelion heads
of spring, and summer's plump
garden hoses. By the time

fall comes around, it seems
like fun was something left soggy
at the bottom of a school bag,

the leaves dry and threatless.
Then, the acorns strut their way
onto the pavement, nicking kids

on the head on their way down.
Even the parents don't mind:
their newspapers, irresistible targets.

It's better than snowballs,
they muster, *better than crabapples.*
And to the kids, it's like the world

has reinvented itself just for them.
Each person: a willing target.
Each kick: a chance for a small riot

to skitter across the unsuspecting lot.
Each hard wind: an opportunity to hit
or be hit, to shake down what's yours.

SEPTOBER IN PHILADELPHIA

Taylor tells me his favorite month is *Septober,*
which he defines as the last two weeks of September
and the first two weeks of October. I like to call it
the Brunch of Autumn, or the impossibly crisp
Heart of Fall, or maybe just the time of the year
when the world becomes sane enough to understand
the flannel importance of pumpkin scones and hot
apple cider, the thrill of seeing your own steamy breath,
the best cup of coffee you'll have tasted in months.
How even the trees shiver brightly, their leaves
refusing to disappear without a stunningly garish fight.

In Philadelphia, you know summer is finally over
when the kids start showing up for football
wearing dark green Eagles hoodies, and the maples
look absolutely drunk with color. It's impossible not
to fall in love in Autumn, and I'm guilty for letting
my jack-o-lantern heart glow for boys who did nothing
more than lob pinecones at my head. Every September,
I'd swear that I would pull off my fantasy: to return
to school so utterly changed, that all the girls I hated
would introduce themselves to me, the pretty new girl,
flattering me with kindness until I open the delicious
secret of voice and say, *See, I told you I could be cool,*
and they'd faint away, shocked and guilty.

I am well past school now, but am still drawn to the Fall,
to clean reams of paper and fresh pens, to that chance
to start over. I've abandoned the wish to reappear
as someone new, but instead am obsessed with being
someone old: that girl who flung herself joy-punched
into leaf piles, who'd eat pumpkin pie with her fingers,

who refused to leave the day for dinner until her cheeks
were bright pink, until that fat sun, nodding his head,
had already zipped up his own dark hoodie
and turned in for the night.

ACKNOWLEDGMENTS

Grateful acknowledgements are made to the following journals in which some of these writings first appeared in slightly different forms:

Crash – "Starling," and "Facts About Seven U.S. Presidents I Still Somehow Remember and the Completely Awful Yet Surprisingly Effective Ways I Remembered Them"

Criminal Class Review – "Polly Wants a Cracker" and "What No One Tells You About Pugs"

Danse Macabre – "Apologies to My Childhood Dog" and "The Youngest Child Lament, Or Moping at the Crossroads"

Dinosaur Bees – "List of Awesome Things You Have to Do"

Fawlt – "Accused"

Frigg Magazine – "Lilith" and "Remembering the Night We Met"

McSweeney's Internet Tendencies: "Sestina For Shappy, Who Doesn't Get Enough Love Poems"

Monkeybicycle - "This Mask Is What's Holding My Face Up"

The Orange Room Review – "Third and Last" and "Our Year of Smut"

Union Station Magazine – "Starter Marriage"

Used Furniture Review – "My Elementary School Confessions." "Times I Wish I Were Funnier" and "After Reading Old Unrequited Love Poems"

Additionally, grateful acknowledgements are made to the following print and audio anthologies, in which some of the following poems have also appeared:

His Rib: Stories, Poems & Essays by Her (Penmanship Books, 2007) – "On Reading Unrequited Love Poems"

Junkyard Ghost Revival (Write Bloody Publishing, 2008) – "Starling"

Learn Then Burn (Write Bloody Press, 2010) – "Ignition" and "Benediction for Prom Night"

Not a Muse: The Inner Lives of Women (New Haven Press, 2009) – "Estephania"

The Last American Valentine (Write Bloody Press, 2008) – "On Reading Unrequited Love Poems" and "How I Spent My Summer Vacations"

Attack of the Urbanabots: Best of NYC-Urbana Slam 2005-2006 (CD) – "Estephania"

Indiefeed Performance Poetry Podcast (performancepoetry.indiefeed.com) – "On Reading Unrequited Love Poems", "Estephania", and "Benediction for Prom Night"

Lastly, grateful acknowledgements are made to **Steve Marsh** and **The Wordsmith Press**, who published an earlier edition of this book.

ABOUT THE AUTHOR

CRISTIN O'KEEFE APTOWICZ is the author of four other books of poetry: *Dear Future Boyfriend, Hot Teen Slut, Working Class Represent,* and *Everything is Everything.* She is also the author of the non-fiction book, *Words In Your Face: A Guided Tour Through Twenty Years of the New York City Poetry Slam,* which *The Washington Post* named as one of five Notable Books on Exploring Poetry in 2008. Born and raised in Philadelphia, Aptowicz moved to New York City at the age of 17. At age 19, she founded the three-time National Poetry Slam championship poetry series NYC-Urbana, which is still held weekly at the NYC's famed Bowery Poetry Club. Most recently, Aptowicz was named the 2010-2011 ArtsEdge Writer-In-Residence at the University of Pennsylvania and was also awarded a 2011 National Endowment for the Arts Fellowship in Poetry.

For more information, please visit her website:
www.aptowicz.com

NEW WRITE BLOODY BOOKS FOR 2011

DEAR FUTURE BOYFRIEND
A Write Bloody reissue of Cristin O'Keefe Aptowicz's first book of poetry

HOT TEEN SLUT
A Write Bloody reissue of Cristin O'Keefe Aptowicz's second book of poetry
about her time writing for porn

WORKING CLASS REPRESENT
A Write Bloody reissue of Cristin O'Keefe Aptowicz's third book of poetry

OH, TERRIBLE YOUTH
A Write Bloody reissue of Cristin O'Keefe Aptowicz's fourth book of poetry
about her terrible youth

38 BAR BLUES
A collection of poems by C.R .Avery

WORKIN' MIME TO FIVE
Humor by Derrick Brown

REASONS TO LEAVE THE SLAUGHTER
New poems by Ben Clark

YESTERDAY WON'T GOODBYE
New poems by Brian Ellis

WRITE ABOUT AN EMPTY BIRDCAGE
New poems by Elaina M. Ellis

THESE ARE THE BREAKS
New prose by Idris Goodwin

BRING DOWN THE CHANDELIERS
New poems by Tara Hardy

THE FEATHER ROOM
New poems by Anis Mojgani

LOVE IN A TIME OF ROBOT APOCALYPSE
New poems by David Perez

THE NEW CLEAN
New poems by Jon Sands

THE UNDISPUTED GREATEST WRITER OF ALL TIME
New poems by Beau Sia

SUNSET AT THE TEMPLE OF OLIVES
New poems by Paul Suntup

GENTLEMAN PRACTICE
New poems by Buddy Wakefield

HOW TO SEDUCE A WHITE BOY IN TEN EASY STEPS
New poems by Laura Yes Yes

OTHER WRITE BLOODY BOOKS (2003 - 2010)

STEVE ABEE, GREAT BALLS OF FLOWERS (2009)
New poems by Steve Abee

EVERYTHING IS EVERYTHING (2010)
New poems by Cristin O'Keefe Aptowicz

CATACOMB CONFETTI (2010)
New poems by Josh Boyd

BORN IN THE YEAR OF THE BUTTERFLY KNIFE (2004)
Poetry collection, 1994-2004 by Derrick Brown

I LOVE YOU IS BACK (2006)
Poetry compilation (2004-2006) by Derrick Brown

SCANDALABRA (2009)
New poetry compilation by Derrick Brown

DON'T SMELL THE FLOSS (2009)
New Short Fiction Pieces By Matty Byloos

THE BONES BELOW (2010)
New poems by Sierra DeMulder

THE CONSTANT VELOCITY OF TRAINS (2008)
New poems by Lea C. Deschenes

HEAVY LEAD BIRDSONG (2008)
New poems by Ryler Dustin

UNCONTROLLED EXPERIMENTS IN FREEDOM (2008)
New poems by Brian Ellis

CEREMONY FOR THE CHOKING GHOST (2010)
New poems by Karen Finneyfrock

POLE DANCING TO GOSPEL HYMNS (2008)
Poems by Andrea Gibson

CITY OF INSOMNIA (2008)
New poems by Victor D. Infante

THE LAST TIME AS WE ARE (2009)
New poems by Taylor Mali

IN SEARCH OF MIDNIGHT: THE MIKE MCGEE HANDBOOK OF AWESOME (2009)
New poems by Mike McGee

OVER THE ANVIL WE STRETCH (2008)
New poems by Anis Mojgani

ANIMAL BALLISTICS (2009)
New poems by Sarah Morgan

NO MORE POEMS ABOUT THE MOON (2008)
NON-Moon poems by Michael Roberts

MILES OF HALLELUJAH (2010)
New poems by Rob "Ratpack Slim" Sturma

SPIKING THE SUCKER PUNCH (2009)
New poems by Robbie Q. Telfer

RACING HUMMINGBIRDS (2010)
New poems by Jeanann Verlee

LIVE FOR A LIVING (2007)
New poems by Buddy Wakefield

WRITE BLOODY ANTHOLOGIES

THE ELEPHANT ENGINE HIGH DIVE REVIVAL (2009)
Poetry by Buddy Wakefield, Derrick Brown,
Anis Mojgani, Shira Erlichman and many more!

THE GOOD THINGS ABOUT AMERICA (2009)
An illustrated, un-cynical look at our American Landscape. Various authors.
Edited by Kevin Staniec and Derrick Brown

JUNKYARD GHOST REVIVAL (2008)
Poetry by Andrea Gibson, Buddy Wakefield, Anis Mojgani,
Derrick Brown, Robbie Q, Sonya Renee and Cristin O'Keefe Aptowicz

THE LAST AMERICAN VALENTINE:
ILLUSTRATED POEMS TO SEDUCE AND DESTROY (2008)
24 authors, 12 illustrators team up for a collection of non-sappy love poetry.
Edited by Derrick Brown

LEARN THEN BURN (2010)
Anthology of poems for the classroom. Edited by Tim Stafford and Derrick Brown.

LEARN THEN BURN TEACHER'S MANUAL (2010)
Companion volume to the *Learn Then Burn* anthology. Includes lesson plans and worksheets for educators.
Edited by Tim Stafford and Molly Meacham.

WWW.WRITEBLOODY.COM

WRITEBLOODY
QUALITY AMERICAN BOOKS

PULL YOUR BOOKS UP BY THEIR BOOTSTRAPS

Write Bloody Publishing distributes and promotes great books of fiction, poetry and art every year. We are an independent press dedicated to quality literature and book design, with an office in Long Beach, CA.

Our employees are authors and artists so we call ourselves a family. Our design team comes from all over America: modern painters, photographers and rock album designers create book covers we're proud to be judged by.

We publish and promote 8-12 tour-savvy authors per year. We are grass-roots, D.I.Y., bootstrap believers. Pull up a good book and join the family. Support independent authors, artists and presses.

Visit us online:
WRITEBLOODY.COM

CPSIA information can be obtained at www.ICGtesting.com
260843BV00001B/4/P